AF073480

THE POINT OF THE STICK

PREVIOUS BOOKS BY NEIL FULWOOD

Poetry
No Avoiding It
Can't Take Me Anywhere
Service Cancelled

THE POINT OF
THE STICK

NEIL FULWOOD

All rights reserved. No part of this work covered by the copyright herein may be reproduced or used in any means – graphic, electronic, or mechanical, including copying, recording, taping, or information storage and retrieval systems – without written permission of the publisher.

Printed by imprintdigital
Upton Pyne, Exeter
www.digital.imprint.co.uk

Typesetting and cover design by The Book Typesetters
hello@thebooktypesetters.com
07422 598 168
www.thebooktypesetters.com

Published by Shoestring Press
19 Devonshire Avenue, Beeston, Nottingham, NG9 1BS
(0115) 925 1827
www.shoestringpress.co.uk

First published 2023
© Copyright: Neil Fulwood
© Author photograph: Dennis Apple

The moral right of the author has been asserted.

ISBN 978-1-915553-43-0

ACKNOWLEDGEMENTS

My thanks to the editors of the following publications where some of these poems, or earlier versions of them, originally appeared: *The High Window, Ink Pantry, Ink Sweat & Tears, Litter, Lothlorien Poetry Journal* and *Medusa's Kitchen*.

The title of this collection is taken from Sir Adrian Boult's handbook on the technique of conducting, published in 1920; it is also the title of a 1971 documentary film on the same subject presented by Boult.

A debt of gratitude is owed to Robert Kenchington and Harry Paterson, my brothers in box sets and partners in crime, for their input and encouragement. Cheers, fellas.

Additional thanks to: Alan Baker, Liz Baugh, Lucy Beckett, Amy Clarke, Matt Fox and everyone at the Organ Grinder, Paula Fulwood, Kathy Kieth, John Lucas, Roy Marshall, Louise Newton and Judith Rose; and to family, friends and comrades.

Dedicated to anyone who has ever played in an orchestra

"There are two golden rules for an orchestra: start together and finish together. The public doesn't give a damn what goes on in between."
Sir Thomas Beecham

"There is an enormous amount of bluff in conducting."
Sir Adrian Boult

"I conduct. And if it works, all the better."
Gennady Rozhdestvensky

CONTENTS

Introduction — 1

The poems — 3

The Maestri — 42

Notes — 44

INTRODUCTION

On 6 June 2023, I wrote an untitled eight-line poem about the conductor Leopold Stokowski and sent it to friends on a Messenger group dedicated to classical music. It was intended as a bit of fun: a "guess the maestro" challenge. They guessed correctly, reported that they'd enjoyed the poem and urged me to send another.

And another.

By the end of the month, at which point the Muse threw her hands up and took a leave of absence, I'd produced a sequence of thirty-nine poems, each one seeking to distill the essence of one of the great maestri, either by alluding to their personality or focusing on a formative moment in their life or career. I have left them untitled; the list at the end of the collection provides a who's who.

Of course, the history of recorded classical music encompasses more than just thirty-nine great conductors. There are plenty of worthy candidates I did not write about – Ernest Ansermet, Vladimir Ashkenazy, Eduard van Beinum, Pierre Boulez, Herbert Blomstedt, Riccardo Chailly, Christoph von Dohnanyi, Antal Doráti, Fabio Luisi, Jean Martinon, Charles Munch and Giuseppe Sinopoli to name but a dozen – partly because I knew too little about some of them, but mainly to avoid the poems becoming repetitive in tone and content.

During June 2023, Riccardo Muti stepped down from his directorship of the Chicago Symphony Orchestra. In an interview for American television he expresses his concern that while the standard of orchestral playing continues to increase, the standard of conductors is slipping.

There are very few up-and-coming maestri on the international stage who embody the dynamic tradition of the Golden Age – although the gentleman whose poem closes the book is a glorious and exciting exception. Thankfully, the wealth of remastered and reissued recordings by the true greats preserves a timeless and essential legacy.

*

The father, they will call him,
of modern conducting:

the man who cut the guy ropes
on the past, detaching the art

from periwigged tradition,
staffs beaten on hard floors.

The man who set the cyanotype
for a century and a half

of maestri – economy of gesture,
communication as a non-verbal act,

score as holy writ, understood
on the deepest, most intimate level.

*

In later life, he will profess to dislike it,
this symphony from a besieged city,
this masterwork of human resilience

score smuggled to the States
on microfiche, spy-story tradecraft
the order of the day. Still, it is his

the American broadcast premiere,
airwaves sending out not only
a symphony but the sense, building

like a storm, of history being made.

*

He would like to think the civil unrest erupting
behind him – the catcalls and responses,
hurled punches and returned blows –
has less to do with his podium presence
than Nijinsky and his stomping Lolitas.

Aloof, unruffled, ramrod straight, he leads
his orchestra through adoration, procession
and glorification until the earth is reborn
in pagan ecstasy … Because damned
if he's wasting seventeen rehearsals.

*

Cough-nudge-wink. There's always
a scintillating bit of gossip, be it
Covent Garden contract shenanigans
or high society *folies à deux,*
shade thrown on the great and the good
or what he said that incensed Seattle.

Weigh that against the litany
of orchestras conducted, countries
visited, a jet-setting lifestyle
before the jet-set even existed.
Maestro of international means:
man of the future. Not to be sniffed at!

*

The accent drifts
from one indeterminate part
of *mittel* Europe to another.

In person, on the podium,
in performance
eccentricities pile up

the score sometimes
little more than a suggestion.

*

The black dog has harried him
through Germany, America, England;
through illness, ill-luck and accident.

The black dog, always ready
for its paw-on-throat moment.

Now, his twilight years flare
into a supernova of creativity,
one definitive interpretation

following another. He towers, legacy
secure, the black dog swindled.

*

From the outset it is evident
that this man facing him,
this uniformed American

will not understand, just as
generations (could he see
ahead) will not understand

or choose not to understand
that the point was neither
collaboration nor appeasement

that the only ideology
was High German culture,
its protection from within.

*

No aficionado of rehearsals
("You know the piece, I know it;
why bother?") and no fan either
of controlled conditions
in recording studios. Live
performance is the key:

audience, venue, the element
of risk; that slipstream moment
of improvisation, orchestra
in freefall with him, audience
and critics in held-breath stasis.

*

For all that he can reduce the sound
of an orchestra to a sigh
or drive it to thunderous denouement

the movement of the baton is millimetric.

For all that his image on album covers
is an exercise in the suppression
of personality, a blanking out of distraction

he is the face of wrath to errant players

a rod-of-iron tyrant
answerable only to the score.

*

So perfectly English
he could have been born
with that knighthood

Victorian in the most distilled
sense of the word. Upright.
A stranger to histrionics.

Stick technique immaculate,
everything given the proper degree
of weight and heft, baton

size of a billiard cue
deployed with a slight
supple turn of the
                      wrist.

*

The man who resigned his position
at the Berlin State Opera
in protest at fascism

the man who voided his contract
with La Scala, Milan
in protest at fascism

who decamped to Buenos Aires
a base of operations
for guest conducting

the freelancer as man of integrity.

*

Granted, he did not follow to the letter
the advice of Richard Strauss
("conduct only with one hand,
the other should be in one's pocket")

nevertheless, made virtue of economy:
conducting as the art of precision,
zen-like focus stanchioned
by Austrian certitude. Gestures

minimal; results definitive.

*

Take an orchestra: one that's a heartbeat
from dissolution, ranks depleted
by conscription and casualties.

Rebuild it: an orchestra of the people.
An orchestra that sets schoolboy
and schoolmarm on equal footing,

where any musical background
is qualification enough. Take an orchestra:

define it; stay with it for a lifetime.

*

His Bruckner is a symphony cycle
for the ages: a definitive statement
on the sacred, the all-too-human
and those terrifying void-like spaces

in between; a treatise on faith
and darkness and the interstices
of the deeply felt and seldom
admitted; a masterclass in agony

and transcendence; an edifice
set in visceral contrast against
our earthly ruins: a cathedral
incandescent with the fear of God.

*

The rock star lifestyle years before
rock stars had the Stones to follow
his example: jet aircraft, yachts,

fast cars. Not that a single Porsche
ever ended its days in a swimming pool,
discipline not allowing for such stuff.

The game-plan was perfection –
always that. The repertoire preserved:
a monument, flawless. A second life.

*

Intended or not, there's a hint
of the vaguely pejorative:
waltzmeister instead of maestro;
the chocolate box evocation
of old Vienna on album covers.

It's too easy, the cloyed recoil
from the Musikverein's opulence.

Listen: done-to-death repertoire
swirls with life, agile
and joyous as it was ever meant to be

with a seriousness of purpose,
a depth, that would befit Bruckner.

*

This steely city, extolled by Rat Pack crooners
("the Wrigley Building ... the Union Stockyard")
is where he has reached the zenith of his career:

a city now defined by its orchestra. Big,
brassy, blazing. A city that dares Vienna,
Salzburg, London to match it. In other words:

his kind of town. They should have twinned it
with Budapest. Too long itinerant, *itthon*
defined by music (geography a game of chance)

he is home now, the ring closed, the circle squared.

itthon (Hungarian) – being 'at home'

*

Beneath the sartorial,
the obdurate resolve
of the guerrilla, iron

discipline of a man
who has known battlefield
and tunnel; has been hunted;

who now in the stasis
between audience falling silent
and thunder of opening bars, flings

the baton over his shoulder
then brings it down
like an act of resistance.

*

The composer-conductor
as two-way street;
highbrow educator
as hep-cat populist.

White tuxedo, bow tie:
podium elegance shot through
with Hollywood cool.
Surface and depth.

He conducts as if possessed
or transported. Mahler
surges through him,
an ecstasy of revelation.

*

Debonair in white silk scarf,
gleam in the eye suggesting
imminent mischief – or at least
the thought of it. Irrepressible:

the maestro as iconoclast –
part professorial, part prankster,
smooth operator at ease
in the robes of elder statesman.

*

Lone wolf in a profession
where iconoclasm's the norm

the 'inspired-but-unpredictable' tag
not a construct of ego or myth-
making but by-product
of bad health and self-doubt

nerves like high-tensile wire
tuned to the agonies
of the great composers.

*

Maestro, choirmaster, organist,
harpsichord virtuoso; workaholic.

Driven; relentless; no quarter
asked of himself or given.

Workloads shouldered in an agony
of against-the-clock momentum.

"My time is now" – *raison d'être*
as epitaph in waiting. Self-discipline

as act of self-destruction.

*

On the podium, he is ursine, intense,
shaggy despite the dinner jacket,
vigorous in shaping the elemental.

Off the podium, a juggernaut
in the struggle for social justice,
tolerance, the attainment of change
through peaceful resolution.

At the stage door, signs programmes,
radiates warmth. "I wish you" –
he beams – "many beautiful things."

*

From the BBC to Sadlers Wells
to Covent Garden: a career path
English enough to beg the word
'quintessential'.   Ah, but …

those wintry explorations of Sibelius
with the Boston Symphony; that headlong
trip with the Concertgebouw
through the *Symphonie Fantastique* …

English? Try otherworldly.

*

Observe: the moment of alchemy
where the slightest of gestures
produces from the orchestra
a coloration or nuance –
a conjuring of the sublime.

Observe: his humanity,
his dignity, apparent in ways
equally understated, equally enigmatic.

*

Mr Hollywood, suave sultan
of the soundtrack; jazz
pianist par excellence; now
maestro, music night popular

career unfolding as a preview
of coming attractions

all the right moves made,
by anybody's definition,
in absolutely the right order.

*

He has racked up stints
with the major American orchestras
the way some guys collect baseball cards

not to mention the heavy-hitters
in Berlin, Vienna, Amsterdam

and now these too-short years
with the LSO, London's finest
elevated to the world's equals

playing fit to beat the devil
but defenceless against
the machinery of fate.

*

It is in his blood:
music, history, nobility

hardwired by decades,
centuries, heritage.

He has resolutely
done his own thing

in absolute service
of the work.

At the close of his career
the *Missa Solemnis* stands,

colossal, a testament.

*

From Airstrip One to Pyongyang
via a departure from Vienna
on point of principle, from

hardball fee demands
to blank-cheque philanthropy,
from lifelong celebrity status

to lack of interest in anything – fame,
adulation, acolytes – except
the music; and even then

wilful enough to make it
as strange and disconcerting
as clocks suddenly striking thirteen.

*

Perhaps the only conductor
in the history of classical music
to demand as payment
a custom-built Audi.

Certainly not the only conductor
to call off appearances, exit
rehearsals in fit of pique.

Arguably the hardest-working
at attaining for the history books
that troubled genius reputation,

justified or not.

*

Baton jinking like a duellist's blade,
podium eschewed, his presence
a physicality of shrugs and tics,
a Pierrot of paranoia

he has been too long at odds
with the system. He wonders sometimes
why he is still alive and allowed
his tenures in the west.

*

The smile is diffident
with maybe a hint
of the impish. In rehearsal,
urges his orchestra:
"listen", yet remains
a man of few words
and those softly spoken.

The eyes communicate
the presence consolidates

the music responds.

*

Regard the still-active octogenarian:
pull back. Regard the maestro helming
the watched-by-millions spectacular
that made football chant of grand opera:
pull back. Regard the flamboyant showman,
core repertoire as Hollywood Bowl swagger:
pull back. Regard the twenty-something
with talent to burn – demoniac in his brilliance:

pull back. Stop here: the music student
who put together his own orchestra,
a refugee camp his debut as maestro,
music given where it was most needed.

*

> *"... oh my country, so beautiful and lost ..."*

File under *finest hour*: in an act
both unorthodox and as utterly Verdi
as it gets, he cuts off *Nabucco*
right after 'Va pensiero',
turns to the audience, preaches

the gospel according to opera *all'italiana*,
the gospel according to a nation's heritage,
the gospel according to every artist
under the stranglehold of government.
Then he cues in the chorus again

choir and audience joining together,
tears in their eyes, hearts beating hard.

*

A touch of the mystic, perhaps,
or the conjuror – someone
in whose hands the unknown,
the forgotten, the rediscovered

are invigorated, burnished,
their reclaimed histories hymned.

A touch of the shaman.
The dreamwoven soul of the poet.
The ageless care of the curator.

*

Where the small-mindedness of politics
evaporates, differences fade, borders
shrink to erasable lines; where, perhaps,
things can be as they should.

Everything is sublimated to the music:
always, the drive to achieve
synthesis of art and possibility,
to set music stands in place of weapons.

*

Nimbly, he has sidestepped
the partisan entrenchments,
the tedium of academic point-scoring;

not for him the gospel of music
as intellectual exercise.

This is period performance
embraced by an ensemble
in concert with his only agenda:

big-hearted exuberance
for the music and all it contains.

*

Moscow St Petersburg London
Armenia Bavaria San Francisco
Munich Vienna   The journey
too long for an ending this tawdry

A plea against violence after Beslan

A memorial for the dead of South Ossetia

A concert for Palmyra at its liberation

And now the falling dominos
of cancellation, meddling fingers
choking the music.

*

In interview, he is charm
itself; enthusiastic
to the point of boyish:

the transformation comes
as he takes the stage

claiming the podium
like a warrior –

it's palpable: a rising,
a deepening; a matter of stature,
aura. An unsurpassed charisma.

THE MAESTRI

Arthur Nikisch
Arturo Toscanini
Pierre Monteux
Sir Thomas Beecham
Leopold Stokowski
Otto Klemperer
Wilhelm Furtwängler
Hans Knappertsbusch
Fritz Reiner
Sir Adrian Boult
Erich Kleiber
Karl Böhm
Sir John Barbirolli
Eugen Jochum
Herbert von Karajan
Willi Boskovsky
Sir Georg Solti
Carlo Maria Giulini
Leonard Bernstein
Sir Neville Marriner
Klaus Tennstedt
Karl Richter
Kurt Masur
Sir Colin Davis

Bernard Haitink
André Previn
Istvan Kertesz
Nikolaus Harnoncourt
Lorin Maazel
Carlos Kleiber
Gennady Rozhdestvensky
Claudio Abbado
Zubin Mehta
Riccardo Muti
Jordi Savall
Daniel Barenboim
Trevor Pinnock
Valery Gergiev
Klaus Mäkelä

NOTES

Page 4. **Arturo Toscanini** conducted the American broadcast premiere of Shostakovich's Leningrad Symphony following the peregrinations of the score (smuggled out of occupied Russia on microfiche) and no small degree of politicking between rival conductors and radio networks.

Page 5. **Pierre Monteux** conducted the premiere of Stravinsky's *Le Sacre du Printemps*. When rioting broke out, Monteux calmly led his orchestra, with whom he had held an unheard of seventeen rehearsals, through the rest of the score.

Page 9. Though never a member of the party or a supporter of its ideology, **Wilhelm Furtwängler** underwent rigorous assessment by a denazification Committee after the war. His rationalisation for remaining in Germany was to protect high German culture from propagandist misuse.

Page 15. When **Sir John Barbirolli** took over the Hallé, its ranks were depleted. He painstakingly rebuilt the orchestra and turned it into a world-class ensemble with whom he remained throughout his career.

Page 20. Drafted into the Italian army in 1940, pacifist and anti-fascist **Carlo Maria Giulini** refused to fire at human targets in battle conditions; he deserted in 1942 and went into hiding, living in subterranean conditions for nine months whilst under an *in absentia* death sentence.

Page 25. **Kurt Masur**'s stage door greeting to fans and autograph hunters is drawn from the author's recollection of meeting him.

Page 29. **Istvan Kertesz**'s partnership with the London Symphony Orchestra looked set to develop into one of the most feted in classical music but was curtailed by his tragic death in a swimming accident.

Page 31. In a career dogged by controversy, **Lorin Maazel** invested large sums of his own money in a production of his now forgotten opera based on George Orwell's *1984*, toured North Korea with the New York Philharmonic, and recorded unorthodox, almost deconstructive accounts of the standard repertoire.

Page 36. On 12 March 2011, **Riccardo Muti** halted a performance of Verdi's *Nabucco* at the Teatro dell'Opera, Rome, to deliver a blistering attack on

Silvio Berlusconi's government, stating: "… this evening, when the choir sang 'oh my country, so beautiful and lost', I thought that if we kill the culture on which is founded the history of Italy, then truly our country *will* be beautiful and lost …" Recommencing the opera at the 'Va pensiero' chorus, the audience joined in with the choir, many of them moved to tears.

Page 38. In 1999, **Daniel Barenboim** and academic Edward Said – of, respectively, Argentinian-Israeli and Palestinian-American backgrounds – founded the West-Eastern Divan Orchestra, named after a collection of poetry by Goethe, with the aim of bringing Arab and Israeli musicians together.

Page 40. Following Vladimir Putin's invasion of the Ukraine in 2022, **Valery Gergiev** – known to be supportive of the Russian president – was dismissed from various positions and/or appearances by the Rotterdam Philharmonic Orchestra, La Scala Milan, Carnegie Hall, the Verbier Festival, the Munich Philharmonic and the Royal Swedish Academy of Music, despite his frequent anti-violence stance and tribute concerts for the victims of war.